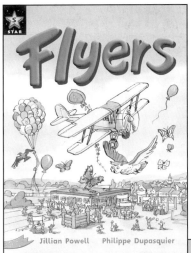

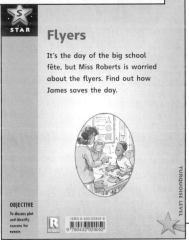

The front cover

Who can read the title?

What can you see in the picture?

What do you think this story is about?

Remember the word 'flyers' has two meanings.

The back cover

Let's read the blurb.

What do you think the book is about?

The title page

What can you see in this picture?

How do you think this boy is feeling?

Why might he be feeling pleased?

The author of this book is Jillian Powell. The illustrator is Philippe Dupasquier.

Lesson 1

READ

Read pages 2 and 3

Purpose: To find out what the class was planning and why.

PAUSE

Pause at page 3

What was the class planning and why? What is the teacher called? What jobs needed to be done?

Look at the picture – is everyone paying attention?

READ

Read pages 4 and 5

Purpose: To find out what Miss Roberts asked James to do, and what he thought she meant.

PAUSE

Pause at page 5

What did Miss Roberts ask James to do? Why did he look a bit shocked? What did he think Miss Roberts meant? What ideas did he have?

Look at the word 'Brainstorm' on page 4.
It is made up of two smaller words – what are they?
A word like this is called a 'compound' word.
Who knows what 'brainstorm' means?

Miss Roberts' class was planning the school fête. They wanted to raise money for homeless children.

"We need to make some signs," said Miss Roberts. "Joe, could you make one for the cake table? Tina, could you make one for the hot dog stand?"

"James," said Miss Roberts, "will you see to the flyers? We'll need lots of them to bring in the crowds. Brainstorm some ideas and then use the computer."

James went to the computer room.

"Where can I find lots of flyers for the school fête?" he thought. Then he had some ideas.

READ

Read pages 6 and 7

Purpose: To find out what James decided to do first.

PAUSE

Pause at page 7

Who knows what an e-mail is? (*It's a way of sending a message through a computer network.*) Who did James send an e-mail to?

How does James feel on page 7?

Find a compound word on page 7. (*airport*)

READ

Read pages 8 and 9

Purpose: To find out who James e-mailed next and what the reply was.

PAUSE

Pause at page 9

Who did James e-mail? What was the reply?

What was James trying to do? Was this what Miss Roberts asked him to do?

How did the other children feel about James in this picture? Why?

Find as many capital letters as you can on pages 8 and 9. As children find capitals, ask them to find reasons why these words have a capital letter, i.e. new sentence, name of person (*James*), name of place (e.g. *the Bird Centre*).

He sent an e-mail to the airport. It said, "Our school is having a fête to raise money for homeless children. Please can you send us an aeroplane?"

Soon an e-mail came back from the airport. "We will see what we can do," it said.
"Yes!" said James.

Then he sent an e-mail to the Bird Centre at the zoo. It said, "Our school is having a fête to raise money for homeless children. Please can you send us some birds to show at the fête?"

An e-mail came back. It said, "We will see what we can do."
"Yes!" said James.

READ

Read pages 10 and 11

Purpose: To find out how James was getting on with the flyers.

PAUSE

Pause at page 11

What did James want to get next for the fête?
Who did he e-mail?

What did Miss Roberts ask James? Can you find her exact words?

What did Miss Roberts think James was doing?
What was he actually doing?

Can you find a compound word on page 10? (*butterfly*)

Turn to page 15 for Revisit and Respond activities.

Then James sent an e-mail to the butterfly farm. He sent an e-mail to the toy shop.

Just then Miss Roberts came in. "How are you getting on with the flyers?" she asked.

"Don't worry, Miss Roberts," said James. "There will be lots of flyers for the school fête."

"Good!" said Miss Roberts.

Lesson 2

RECAP

Recap lesson 1

What did Miss Roberts (the teacher) ask James to do?

What did James think she meant?

Why did James get confused?

What do you think is going to happen on the day of the school fête?

READ

Read pages 12 to 15

Purpose: To find out why Miss Roberts was worried and who had arrived at the school fête.

PAUSE

Pause at page 15

What was the problem at the school fête? Was James worried? Which sentence tells us that?

Who was at the fête? What do they have in common?

Can you find a compound word on page 15? (*overhead*)

The day of the school fête came. James was pleased because the flyers had arrived. Miss Roberts was worried because very few people had arrived.

There was a man from the butterfly farm with lots of colourful butterflies. There was a woman from the toy shop with balloons and kites.

There was a man feeding an owl that sat on his hand. There was a small aeroplane buzzing overhead.

READ

Read pages 16 and 17

Purpose: To find out what Miss Roberts suddenly realizes.

PAUSE

Pause at page 17

How did Miss Roberts feel when she saw the pilot? Which word tells you this? (*crossly*)

What did Miss Roberts realize had happened? How do you think she feels? And how might James feel? What do you think they could do about it?

Find the word 'publicity'. What does it mean?

READ

Read pages 18 to 21

Purpose: To find out what good idea James had.

Suddenly the aeroplane landed in the school playing field. The pilot got out.

"Just what do you think you are doing?" said Miss Roberts crossly.

"He's one of the flyers," said James.

"What do you mean, James?" asked Miss Roberts. Then she saw the butterflies, the kites and the birds.

"Oh, James," she said, "I didn't mean that kind of flyers. I meant publicity flyers to let people know about the fête!"

"I have an idea!" said James.

And he ran over to the school fence.

James came back carrying the school fête banner. He gave it to the pilot.

PAUSE

Pause at page 21

What was James's plan? Where did he get the banner from? What do you think will happen when people see the banner?

Why do you think the banner was written in capital letters?

READ

Read pages 22 to the end

Purpose: To find out if James's plan worked so that the school fête was a success.

James and the pilot climbed into the aeroplane and took off. A big banner flew out behind the aeroplane. It said, "Come to the most amazing school fête ever!"

Lots of people saw the banner and came to the school fête.

The school raised lots of money for homeless children. Television people came to see James. They asked about the flyers.

"This is the best school fête we've had," said Miss Roberts. "With some of the best flyers ever. Well done, James!"

24

PAUSE

Pause at page 24

What happened when people saw the banner?

Was the school fête a success? What things tell you this? (*crowds at the fête, television interest, large amount of money raised*)

What does Miss Roberts say to James at the end? What do you think she means by 'the best flyers ever'?

How do you think Miss Roberts and James feel at the end?

After Reading

Revisit and Respond

Lesson 1

T Identify and discuss reasons for events in the story so far. Ask the children, in groups, to write down possible endings to the story.

S Ask the children when capital letters are used. Ask them to find examples in the text to back up suggestions (e.g. the beginning of sentences, names, etc.).

W Ask the children what a compound word is. List the compound words they have already found in the text (e.g. *brainstorm, airport, butterfly*). Ask them to brainstorm more (e.g. *seaside, railway, scarecrow*).

Lesson 2

T Look at the possible endings written by the group last time. Compare with the actual ending in the book. What are the similarities and differences?

T Ask children, in a group, to discuss what sort of things need to be included in a flyer (e.g. what's happening, where, when). Make a list. Encourage them to think of the layout, language used and design.

S As part of the work for the 'flyer', think about sentence structure, use of capitals, punctuation, etc.

W Discuss with children, as part of the work for the 'flyer', some appropriate words for the flyer (e.g. *brilliant, fantastic, amazing*).

Follow-up

Independent Group Activity Work

This book is accompanied by two photocopy masters, one with a reading focus, and one with a writing focus, which support the main teaching objectives of this book. The photocopy masters can be found in the Planning and Assessment Guide.

PCM 23 (*reading*)

PCM 24 (*writing*)

Writing

Guided writing: Design and write a flyer for a school event. Use PCM 24.

Extended writing: Write a story about something that happened at your school fête.

Assessment Points

Assess that the children have learnt the main teaching points of the book by checking that they can:

- identify and discuss reasons for events in stories
- predict the ending of the story
- identify compound words and split them into their component parts.